# EYE SPY

# EYE
## SPY

WORLD BOOK, INC.

CHICAGO LONDON SYDNEY TORONTO

World Book, Inc.
525 W. Monroe
Chicago, IL 60661
U.S.A.

Cover design: Design 5

ISBN: 0-7166-4102-X

For information on other World Book
products, call **1-800-255-1750, X2238.**

Printed in Mexico

1 2 3 4 5 99 98 97 96

# Introduction

In most of the puzzles in this book, you have to look for something that's hidden. It may be a word that's hidden in the names of pictures. It may be two things that are just alike, hidden among a lot of things that look different. Or, there may be two things that are different, hidden among a lot of things that look alike. But, whatever it is, the best way to find it is by *looking* very carefully.

# Hidden sides

1. No matter how you look at a cube, such as
   a building block, you can see only three
   sides of it. How many sides (including top
   and bottom) does a cube have altogether?

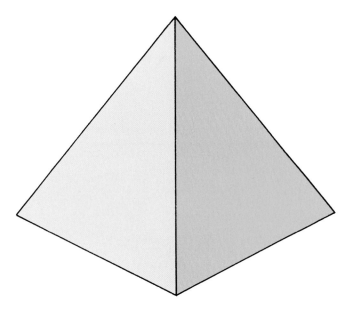

2. How many sides, including the bottom, does this pyramid have? Here's a hint—the back of the pyramid looks just like the front.

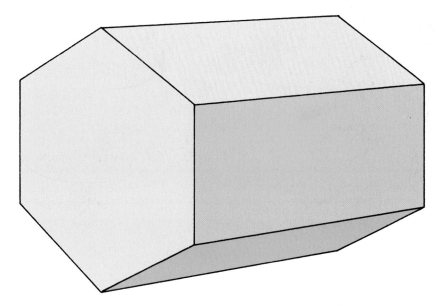

3. How many sides, including top and bottom, does this shape have? The back looks just like the front.

(ANSWERS ON PAGE 29)

# Strange sights!

There are a great many strange things going on in this picture! Can you find them all?

(ANSWERS ON PAGE 29)

# The last acorn

For weeks, Fletcher Squirrel has been gathering acorns. Now, there is only one acorn left. Can you show Fletcher which branch leads to the acorn? And remember, it's not fair to jump from one branch to another!

(ANSWER ON PAGE 29)

# Which balloon?

The little girl has just bought a balloon.
The monkey is handing her the string.
Which balloon is attached to the string?

(ANSWER ON PAGE 30)

# Picture-words

The first letters in the names of the objects in each row can be put together to make a word. When the three words are put together, they make a sentence. What is the sentence?

(ANSWER ON PAGE 30)

# Where's Rover?

The children's dog is lost in the middle of the lumberyard! Can you show them which path they have to take to find him?

(ANSWER ON PAGE 30)

# Ladybugs, ladybugs

Which two ladybugs look exactly alike?

(ANSWER ON PAGE 30)

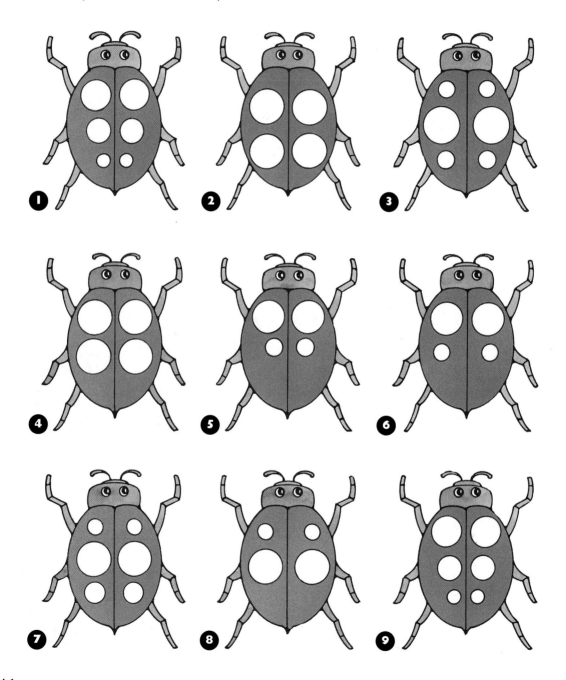

# Ollie the Octopus

Which shadow exactly matches Ollie's picture?

(ANSWER ON PAGE 30)

# Finish the picture

Four pieces are missing from this picture. They
are mixed up with others, below. Can you find
the right pieces and put them where they belong?

(ANSWERS ON PAGE 31)

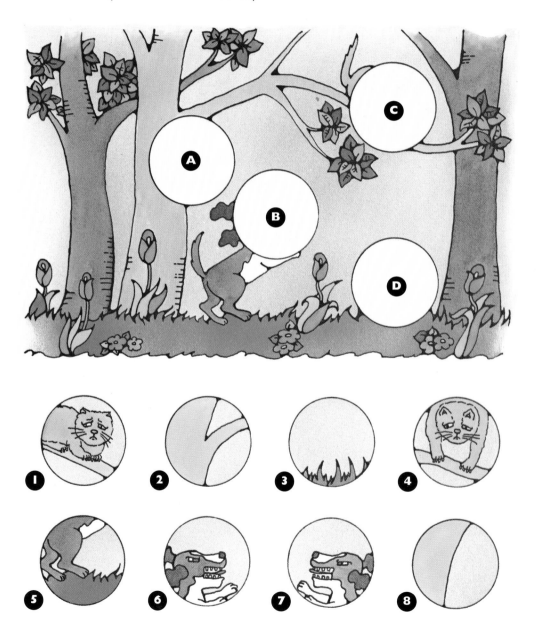

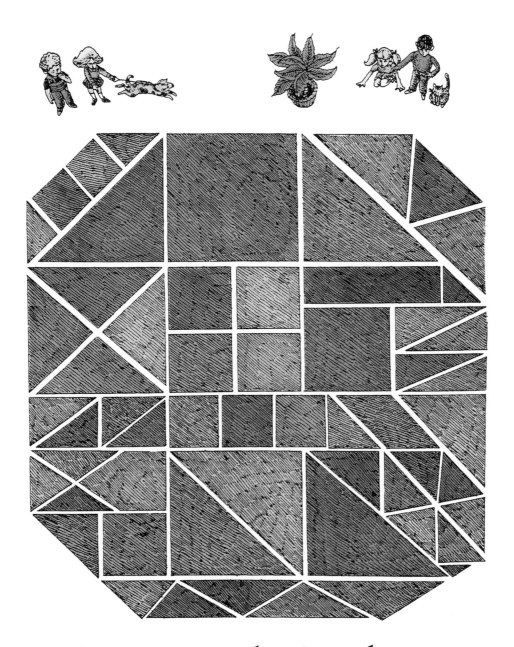

# Squares and triangles

Hidden among all the squares and triangles are
three shapes that are *not* squares or triangles.
Can you find them?

(ANSWERS ON PAGE 31)

# Mixed-up snakes

One of these five snakes is different from all the others. Can you find it?

(ANSWER ON PAGE 31)

# What's wrong?

There's something wrong with each of these pictures. Do you know what it is?

(ANSWERS ON PAGE 32)

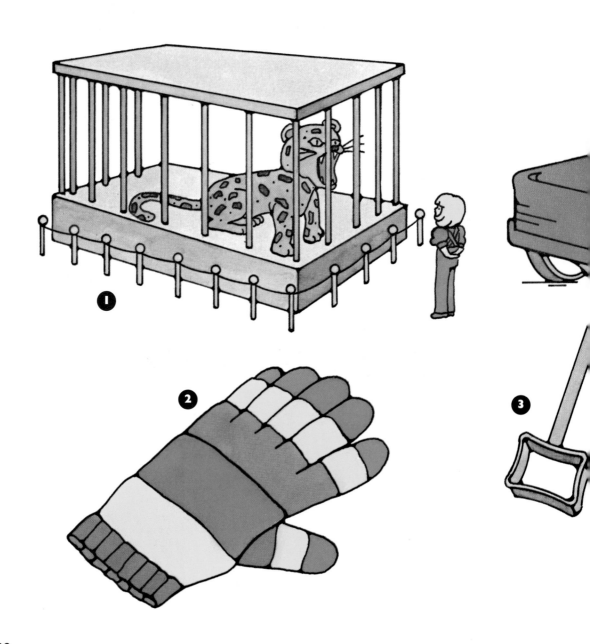

**4**

**5**

# Eye foolers

The things on these pages are all "eye foolers." You may have to look at them in different ways to find the answers.

(ANSWERS ON PAGE 32)

1. Find the missing piece of pie.

2. Which alligator's eye is closest to the middle alligator's eye?

3. Which elf is the tallest?

4. What does this say?

HERE'S LOOKING AT YOU, KID

# Strange shapes

The picture above shows a desk in an office.
There are many objects on the desk. Each object is
labeled with a letter. Each picture on the opposite
page shows part of each object. Can you match
them up? Here's a hint—number 1 is part of E.

(ANSWERS ON PAGE 32)

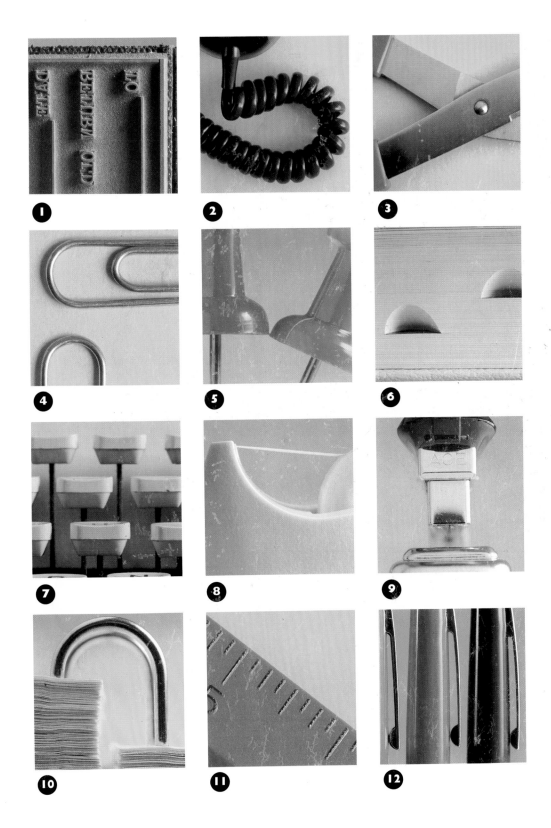

# More strange shapes

The pictures below are really nothing more than parts of common, everyday objects. Can you figure out what each one is?

(ANSWERS ON PAGE 32)

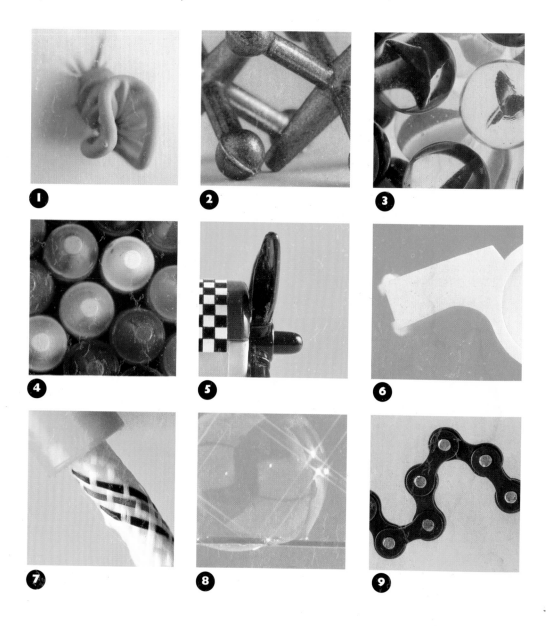

## Hidden sides (PAGE 6)

1. A cube has six sides, including the top and bottom.
2. A pyramid has five sides, including the bottom.
3. This shape has eight sides, including the top and bottom.

# Answers

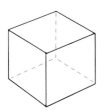 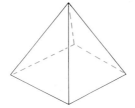 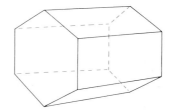

## Strange sights (PAGE 8)

The strange sights are shown in blue.

## The last acorn (PAGE 10)

# Answers

## Which balloon?
(PAGE 12)

## Picture-words (PAGE 13)

*h*elicopter, *o*wl, *w*indmill:  how
*a*pple, *r*hinoceros, *e*gg:  are
*y*o-yo, *o*strich, *u*mbrella:  you

## Where's Rover?
(PAGE 14)

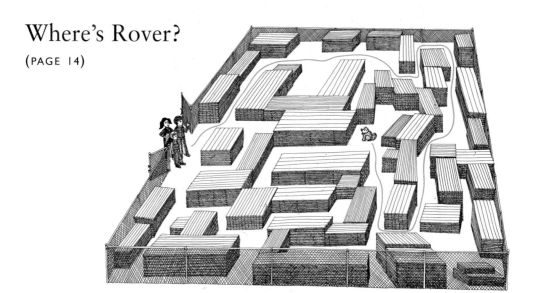

## Ladybugs, ladybugs (PAGE 16)
Numbers 1 and 9 are the same.

## Ollie the Octopus (PAGE 17)
Ollie's shadow is number 5.

# Answers

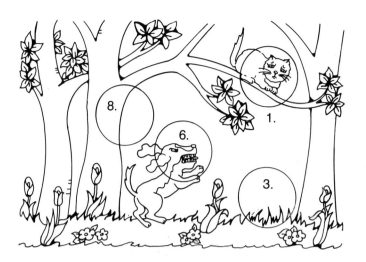

Finish the picture
(PAGE 18)

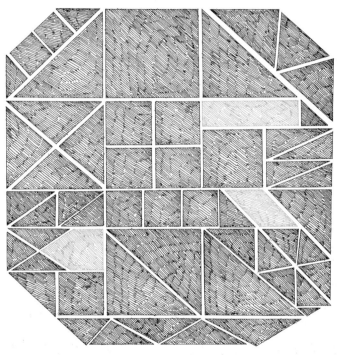

Squares and
triangles
(PAGE 19)

Mixed-up
snakes (PAGE 20)

# Answers

## What's wrong? (PAGE 22)

1. There are no bars on the back of the cage.
2. The glove has six fingers.
3. The body of the wagon is upside down.
4. The pedals are on the back wheel of the bicycle.
5. The grape juice is in the upper part of the glass.

## Eye foolers (PAGE 24)

1. Turn the picture upside down and you'll see the piece of pie.
2. The eyes of both alligators are exactly the same distance from the middle alligator's eye.
3. The elf at the left is the tallest.
4. To read this, hold the edge of the book level with your eyes. If you move the book slightly, you'll see the words. They say: Here's looking at you, kid.

## Strange shapes (PAGE 26)

1—E: rubber stamp
2—D: telephone cord
3—I: scissors
4—L: paper clips
5—F: pushpins
6—G: edge of book
7—J: typewriter keys
8—C: transparent tape and dispenser
9—B: stapler
10—A: desk calendar
11—H: ruler
12—K: pen

## More strange shapes (PAGE 28)

1. tied end of balloon
2. jacks
3. marbles
4. crayons
5. model airplane propeller
6. mouth of whistle
7. bottom of jump rope and handle
8. soap bubble and bubble ring
9. bicycle chain